How We Move

Rufus Bellamy

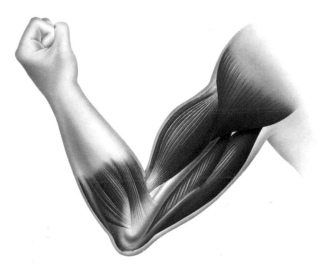

W

FRANKLIN WATTS

This edition 2007

Franklin Watts
338 Euston Road, London NW1 3BH

Franklin Watts Australia
Level 17/207 Kent Street
Sydney, NSW 2000

Series editor: Adrian Cole
Series design: White Design
Art director: Jonathan Hair
Picture research: Diana Morris
Educational consultant: Beverley Goodger
Medical consultant: Dr Gabrielle Murphy

A CIP catalogue record for this book is available from the British Library.

ISBN–13: 978 0 7496 7255 3

Printed in Malaysia

Acknowledgements:
John Bavosi/SPL: 7t. Alain Dex/Publiphoto Diffusion/SPL: 29t.
Duomo/Corbis: front cover, 5t. FK Photo/Corbis: 22c. Laurence
Fordyce/Eye Ubiquitous/Corbis: 9b. Astrid & Hanns Frieder Michler/
SPL: 17cr. Adam Hart-Davis/SPL: 14b. Robin Hume/Sporting Pictures: 5b.
David Katzenstein/Corbis: 15b. Louvre, Paris/Bridgeman Art Library:
10b. Joe Mann/Sporting Pictures: 29b. Roy Morsch/Corbis: 21b.
Richard T Nowitz/Corbis: 21t. Cristina Pedrazzini/SPL: 8b. Quest/
SPL: 11cr. Giovanni Reda/Corbis: 19t. Ariel Skelley/Corbis: 27b.
Paul A Souders/Corbis: 12b. David Turnley/Corbis: 7b.
Every attempt has been made to clear copyright.
Should there be any inadvertent omission,
please apply to the publisher for rectification.

Franklin Watts is a division of Hachette Children's Books.

Contents

The body moves using
muscle pulling power

Frontalis
wrinkles the
forehead

Orbicularis oris
purses the lips

Deltoid
moves shoulder
and upper arm

Pectoralis major
rotates and pulls
arm towards body

Biceps brachii
bends arm at
the elbow

Rectus abdominis
pulls in
abdomen

Rectus femoris
straightens knee

Sartorius
bends and
turns leg

Tibialis anterior
turns and lifts foot

The human body is capable of an amazing variety of movements, from the smallest twitch to the largest leap. To make such movements happen, the brain sends impulses to particular muscles. When the muscles receive these impulses they contract. The muscles pull on the parts of the body that they are attached to and make them move. This is how all the movements that make us run, wave or smile are made.

Muscles for movement

Muscles are almost always attached to bones. Bones make up the strong framework inside the body – the skeleton. It is the way in which bones and muscles are arranged that allows us to move in the ways we can.

Energy for action

Movement needs a lot of energy and this comes from the food we eat. The digested food chemicals that contain the energy are carried in the blood to the muscles. Once the chemicals get to the muscles the energy is released and is used to make the muscles contract.

Muscles revealed

The skin and fat have been stripped away so that we can see some of the body muscles. They provide the pulling force for all the movements that the body makes.

Keeping moving

We should not take movement for granted. Illness or accidents can stop us moving. If we only move a little it can be bad for our health. But if we exercise regularly we can become fitter and healthier.

Riding high

This BMX trick is performed using a number of perfectly co-ordinated, complex movements. Movement is vital to everyday life – and having fun.

IT'S AMAZING!

To see just how amazing people are at moving, take a look at some movement records. The men's world record for the 100 metre sprint is 9.78 seconds and the women's is 10.49 seconds – that is about the time it takes to read this sentence. People are just as good at controlling their movements so that they do not move. The world record for standing still is over 20 hours!

Even non-record holders are amazing movers. The number of steps an average person makes in their lifetime would carry them at least twice round the world. In the same time, that person would also blink their eyes about 250 million times.

Explosive run

Athletes compete in track events using exactly the same muscles as someone does when running for a bus.

The body has many
flexible joints

The skeleton is the bony framework inside the body. Where the skeleton's bones meet there are joints. In some joints, such as those in the skull, the bones fit so tightly together that little or no movement is possible. In other joints, such as those in the shoulders and knees, the bones are connected together so that they can move freely. These are called synovial joints.

Scapula
shoulder blade

The flexible shoulder

The shoulder contains a joint in which the round head of one bone (the humerus) sits in a smooth hole in another bone (the scapula). This ball and socket joint allows the arm to move freely in all directions.

Synovial joints

There are several different types of synovial joint. Each type connects bones in a different way and allows different sorts of movement. We can whirl our arms around like propellers because of the ball and socket joints in our shoulders. But we can only bend our knees backwards and forwards. This is because the knees contain hinge joints.

Ball and socket joint

This type of joint allows movement in several directions. Ball and socket joints occur in the shoulder and the hip.

Humerus
upper
arm bone

Reducing friction

Parts of an engine need oil to move smoothly. Synovial joints move smoothly because they produce their own oily substance called synovial fluid. This fluid lubricates the joints and reduces friction inside them – without it the joints would not be able to move as easily.

Absorbing shock

Synovial joints can be put under a lot of stress, for example when we jump or run. Strong, flexible fibres called ligaments hold the bones together and prevent them becoming dislocated. Cartilage protects the ends of the bones in these joints. It is a smooth, tough material that is softer than bone. Some synovial joints, such as those in the knees, also contain discs of cartilage that help absorb shock and protect the joints. Other joints contain small sacs of fluid called bursae. These act as a cushion at pressure points like those found at the elbows.

Hinge joint

Hinge joints occur in the knee, shown here, the elbow and fingers. This type of joint only allows movement backwards and forwards.

Synovial membrane produces synovial fluid

Cartilage helps absorb pressure

Ligament holds the joint together

Stretching exercises
Dancers do special stretching exercises to achieve a high level of flexibility.

CAN YOU BE DOUBLE-JOINTED?

If someone says they are 'double-jointed' it usually means that they can bend their fingers in funny ways, or can put their feet behind their head. Such people do not really have double joints, they can just move the bones in their joints more than most people.

It is possible to increase flexibility – the amount you can move your joints – by doing special stretching exercises. These are part of a dancer's training. They should only be done with advice from an expert as they can cause injury if done incorrectly.

Movements are made using
muscles, bones and joints

We make almost all movements using our muscles, bones and joints. To lift a cup to the mouth, the brain sends a nerve impulse to the muscle on the front of the upper arm (the biceps), which pulls on the bones in the forearm as it contracts. Because the elbow contains a hinge joint, the pull from the muscle makes the arm bend.

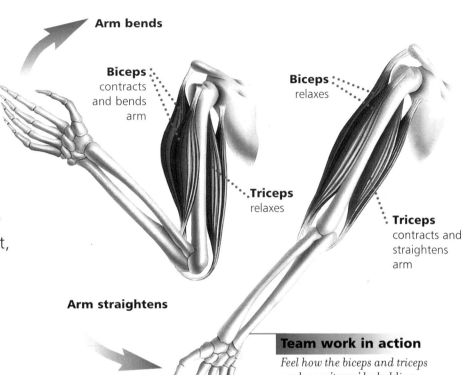

Arm bends

Biceps
contracts and bends arm

Triceps
relaxes

Biceps
relaxes

Triceps
contracts and straightens arm

Arm straightens

Team work in action
Feel how the biceps and triceps work as a 'team' by holding the front and back of your upper arm while bending and straightening the arm.

Muscle teams

Muscles only pull – they cannot push. So, muscles work in teams to produce all the different movements we can make. The biceps, for example, can only bend the arm, it cannot straighten it. This is done by the muscle at the back of the upper arm (the triceps). When the triceps muscle pulls, the biceps relaxes and the arm straightens. The triceps and biceps are called 'antagonists' because one pulls while the other relaxes.

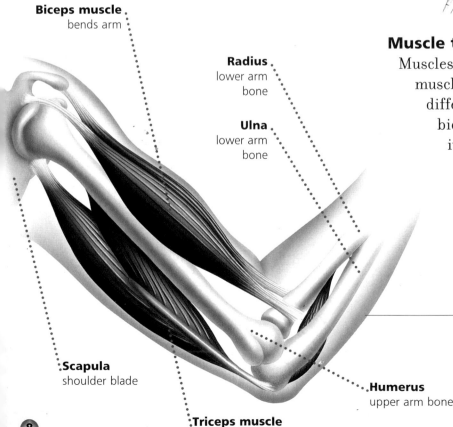

Biceps muscle
bends arm

Radius
lower arm bone

Ulna
lower arm bone

Scapula
shoulder blade

Triceps muscle
straightens arm

Humerus
upper arm bone

Pulling produces movement
The biceps is attached to the shoulder blade (the scapula) and the radius bone in the forearm. Because the scapula is normally held steady by the rest of the body, when the biceps contracts the forearm moves.

Movements and levers

The way the bones, joints and muscles are linked and move is very important. The arm, for example, is arranged so that a small movement of the biceps or triceps pivots the forearm bones (the ulna and radius) around the elbow joint and produces a much bigger movement of the hand.

The forearm bones act as a lever, a rigid rod that moves on a fixed point called a fulcrum (in this example the elbow joint). The bones transfer the pulling force of the arm muscles. This is only one example of a lever in the body. These levers are very important — if we did not have them we would not be able to do many of the things that we take for granted (see below).

Movement of hand

Pull from muscles

Fulcrum

A living lever

The force of the muscles counter-acts the weight of the hand and so moves the hand upwards.

A lever in action

The wheelbarrow and a foot act as levers. The weight lies between the fulcrum and the force.

TWO BODY LEVERS

The skull acts as a lever. It turns on the neck joint and transfers the pulling force of the muscles (splenius capitis) at the back of the neck to lift the weight of the front of the head. Just like a playground see-saw, it pivots on a fulcrum lying between a force and a weight.

The foot also acts as a lever. It turns on the joints between the toes and the body of the foot and transfers the pulling force of the muscles (gastrocnemius and soleus) attached to the back of the foot to lift the weight of the body. Just like a wheelbarrow, it helps lift a weight that lies between an upward force and a fulcrum.

Movement requires
skeletal muscles

There are more than 600 muscles in the human body. These muscles, which have very different functions, fit into three main categories: cardiac muscle provides the vital pumping force in the heart; smooth muscle lines the digestive system and blood vessels; skeletal muscles provide the pull that makes us move. Skeletal muscles make up 35–45 per cent of the weight of an adult human. They also keep the body upright, and with the help of the framework of the skeleton, give the body its shape.

Skeletal muscles

Skeletal muscles are also called voluntary muscles because they are consciously controlled by the brain. When we decide to kick a ball, for example, the brain sends nerve impulses to the correct skeletal muscles in the legs.

Trapezius
pulls head and shoulders backwards

Triceps brachii
straightens arm

Latissimus dorsi
pulls arm down and back

Gluteus maximus
straightens thigh

Flexor carpi ulnaris
moves hand

Gastrocnemius
bends the knee and the foot down

Biceps femoris
bends leg

Soleus
bends foot down

Achilles tendon
links the gastrocnemius to the heel

What's in a name?
Skeletal muscles, like these on the back of the body, all have special Latin names – each plays its part in helping the body to move.

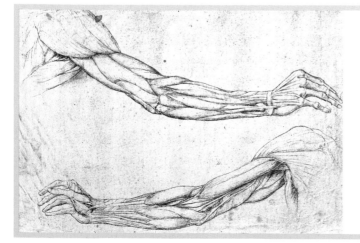

AN EARLY MUSCLE MAN
One of the first people to study muscles properly was the great Italian artist, scientist and inventor Leonardo da Vinci (1452–1519). His drawings of the muscles of living and dead people – made over 500 years ago – are incredibly detailed and accurate. He also made many important observations of the workings of human muscles.

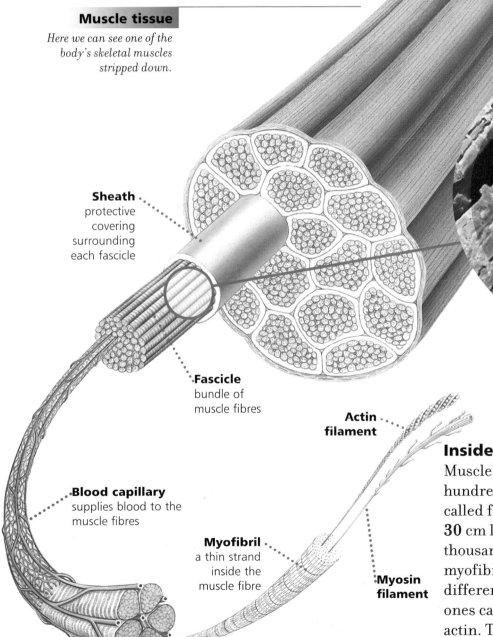

Many different muscles

Skeletal muscles come in all shapes and sizes, and each has its own Latin name, for example gluteus maximus means 'great buttock'. All skeletal muscles have a fleshy central part called the belly. They are also covered in a strong outer layer of tissue called the epimysium. At the ends of many muscles there are very strong non-elastic cords – called tendons – which attach the muscles to bones and also to other muscles.

Whole muscle ·
muscles are made up of bundles of fascicles

Muscle tissue

Here we can see one of the body's skeletal muscles stripped down.

Sheath ·
protective covering surrounding each fascicle

Fascicle
bundle of muscle fibres

Blood capillary
supplies blood to the muscle fibres

Myofibril ·
a thin strand inside the muscle fibre

Actin ·
filament

Myosin
filament

Tissue close-up

This micrograph shows the parallel pattern of the myofibrils found inside the muscle fibre.

Inside a muscle

Muscle tissue is made of bundles of hundreds of thousands of muscle cells called fibres. These fibres are up to **30** cm long. Each one is made of thousands of thinner strands called myofibrils, which are made out of two different types of protein filament: thick ones called myosin and thin ones called actin. These proteins hold the key to how muscles work and how we move.

Muscles work by
contracting and relaxing

A muscle contracts and pulls when it receives nerve impulses from the brain. These impulses trigger chemical reactions in the muscle. The reactions make and break connections between special parts of the muscle's fibres, making the fibres – and the muscle – get shorter.

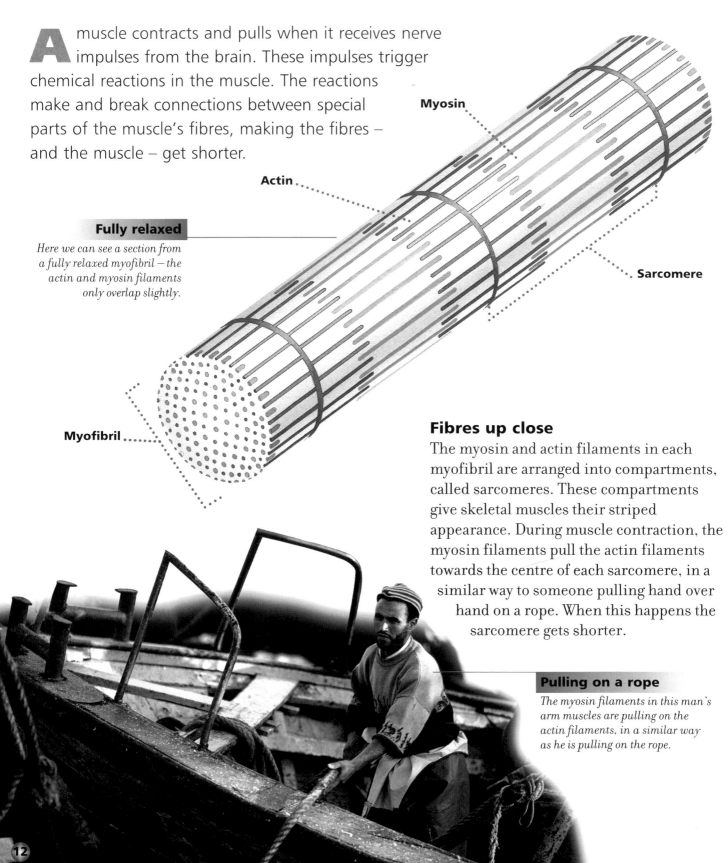

Myosin

Actin

Sarcomere

Fully relaxed

Here we can see a section from a fully relaxed myofibril – the actin and myosin filaments only overlap slightly.

Myofibril

Fibres up close

The myosin and actin filaments in each myofibril are arranged into compartments, called sarcomeres. These compartments give skeletal muscles their striped appearance. During muscle contraction, the myosin filaments pull the actin filaments towards the centre of each sarcomere, in a similar way to someone pulling hand over hand on a rope. When this happens the sarcomere gets shorter.

Pulling on a rope

The myosin filaments in this man's arm muscles are pulling on the actin filaments, in a similar way as he is pulling on the rope.

SEE YOUR MUSCLES IN ACTION

To see muscles at work, ask a friend to relax their arm so that it is straight (the biceps is relaxed, but the triceps is contracted). Then, using a tape measure, measure the distance round the middle of the upper arm (its circumference).

Now ask them to flex their arm until the biceps is fully contracted. Measure round the upper arm again.

What has happened to the circumference of the upper arm? The circumference has increased. This is because as the biceps contracts and its myosin and actin filaments slide past each other and overlap more, the muscle gets shorter and fatter.

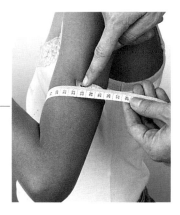

Big muscles

Use a tape measure to see your muscles at work.

Fully contracted

In the fully contracted myofibril, the myosin filaments have pulled the actin filaments to the centre of the sarcomere. The whole myofibril has become shorter.

Receiving impulses

All the sarcomeres in the muscle fibre contract at the same time, making the whole muscle shorter. If the muscle continues to receive nerve impulses it contracts until it reaches its shortest possible length. When the nerve impulses stop the muscle relaxes and returns to its resting length.

The body needs
energy for action

The body is like any machine; it needs energy to move. We get our energy from the food we eat. Food goes into the stomach and intestines, where chemicals produced by the body break the food down into microscopic pieces. These are taken into the blood and carried to the cells.

Energy store

Glucose is a kind of sugar found in certain types of food. Our cells use glucose to make a chemical called ATP (adenosine triphosphate) in tiny structures, called mitochondria. ATP is a vital energy store for movement. It provides the energy that enables myosin filaments to pull on actin filaments and so make muscles contract. Muscle cells contain lots of mitochondria, so that they can make lots of ATP.

A mitochondrion

Mitochondria are the 'powerhouses' inside all our cells – here you can see the production of ATP by aerobic respiration.

ATP is produced by aerobic respiration and used to make muscles contract

Oxygen is taken into the lungs in the air we breathe

Glucose is an energy-rich substance taken into the body in food

Aerobic respiration

When we make less strenuous movements, such as walking, ATP is made using a chemical reaction that requires oxygen. The oxygen comes from the air we breathe via our lungs and is carried to the muscles in the blood. This way of making ATP is called aerobic respiration. It produces heat (which increases body temperature), water and carbon dioxide (which is breathed out).

A hot shot

When muscles contract a lot of energy is released as heat. In this thermogram hot areas are white and yellow.

Anaerobic respiration

When we move very quickly for long periods, for example when we run a long way fast, then not enough energy can be provided by aerobic respiration. When this happens a different chemical reaction takes place – one that produces ATP without oxygen. This is called anaerobic respiration. Unfortunately, this produces a poison called lactic acid, which collects in the muscles. Lactic acid is the reason people's legs feel so tired when they exercise for long periods.

A balanced diet

Glucose is used to power movement. The main source of glucose in our diet is from foods called carbohydrates, which include bread, rice, pasta and potatoes. Between 55 and 60 per cent of the food we eat should be made up of these types of food, so that we have enough energy for all our daily activities.

However, most people agree it is important to eat a balanced diet. A diet containing fruit, dairy foods, water, meat, nuts, vegetables and carbohydrates will ensure the body gets all the chemicals it needs to stay fit, grow and repair itself.

Building a healthy diet

This food pyramid gives a good rough guide to how much of each food we should eat.

CHANGES WITH EXERCISE

When we exercise or move energetically a number of changes take place in our bodies. We breathe faster and take in more air on each breath. Our hearts beat faster and more strongly. The way our blood flows around our bodies also changes so that our muscles receive more blood every minute (see page 27 for more details of this). All these changes take place so that our muscles receive enough oxygen (which is carried in the blood) to make the ATP they need to keep contracting and driving the body's movements.

Practising breathing

Students of karate practise breathing control as part of their training. This helps them to be active for longer.

Body movement is controlled by
nerve impulses

Skeletal muscles do not contract on their own. They only pull when they receive a nerve impulse. However, the body uses two ways to control movement – one uses the brain directly, the other does not. For example, moving a hand to catch a ball requires careful thought, but moving it away quickly after touching hot water seems to happen automatically.

Using the brain

When we decide to move, the brain sends a message to the muscles that must contract. This message is a tiny electrical impulse that travels along a nerve. Nerves are a bit like electrical wires. They run from the brain, along the spinal cord in the back, and spread out all over the body (see left). When a nerve impulse from the brain gets to a muscle, for example in the arm, chemicals are released which cause the muscle fibres to contract.

The nervous system

Nerves run from the brain down the spinal cord to link up with the whole of the body.

Brain
sends impulses to
the muscles

**Motor
nerve cell**
carries impulses
from the brain to
the muscles

Spinal cord
bundles of nerves
that carry impulses

A nerve impulse

Here the brain sends an impulse to the arm muscle to make it contract, but the brain can send impulses all over the body at the same time.

Quick reflexes

Sometimes we need to move very quickly. If we touch something hot with a hand, for example, the body senses pain. A nerve impulse is sent in a few thousandths of a second from the hand to the spinal cord. Here, the impulse takes a short cut. Instead of going to the brain, the nerve impulse passes straight to the muscles that contract and move the hand. This is called a reflex action. Only after the hand has moved does a signal reach the brain to tell it what has happened.

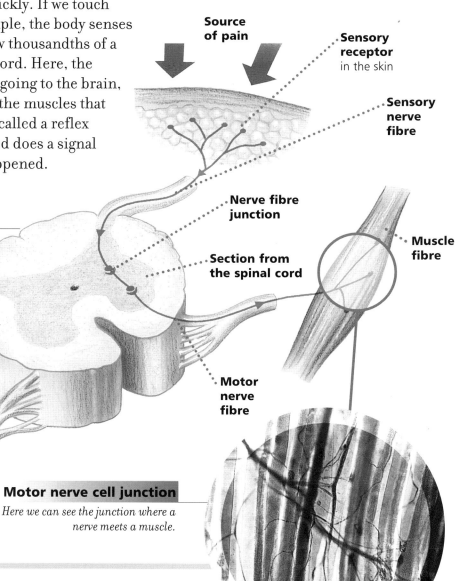

Source of pain

Sensory receptor in the skin

Sensory nerve fibre

Nerve fibre junction

Section from the spinal cord

Muscle fibre

Motor nerve fibre

A reflex pathway
This is how a nerve impulse takes a short cut to create a reflex action.

Stronger movements

The strength of movement produced by a nerve impulse depends on the number of muscle fibres that are made to contract. It also depends on how many nerve impulses reach the muscle in a given time. Muscles only contract when they get nerve impulses; if these stop they relax.

Motor nerve cell junction
Here we can see the junction where a nerve meets a muscle.

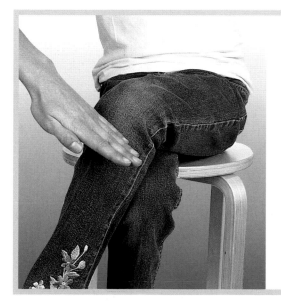

TEST YOUR REFLEXES

You can see a reflex action take place. Get a friend to sit and cross their legs at the knee. Then tap them (gently!) just below the knee. Their leg should jerk up. This reflex action happens because the tap below the knee causes the thigh muscle to stretch. As a result, a nerve impulse is sent from the thigh muscle to the spinal cord and returns to the thigh muscle along another nerve. The returning impulse causes the thigh muscle to contract and the knee jerks.

Movement is co-ordinated by
receptors and senses

Many movements, such as hand clapping, may seem like simple things to do, but they involve many different muscles. Co-ordinating such movements is something we learn to do as children.

Knowing where we are

To make our actions accurate and smooth the brain has to know where all the different parts of the body are and the way in which they are moving. It gets a lot of this information from nerve impulses sent by special cells in our muscles, tendons and joints. These cells are called stretch receptors. They provide information about the position of the body, and help to control movement and keep us upright.

Semicircular canals
three tubes filled with liquid

Cupula
contains hair cells that detect movement in the fluid in the semicircular canals. It sends nerve impulses to the brain

Vestibular nerve
carries balance information to the brain

Vestibule
contains the utricle and saccule that sense gravity

Cochlea
turns sounds into nerve impulses

Cochlear nerve
carries hearing information to the brain

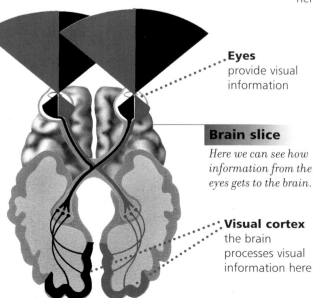

Eyes
provide visual information

Brain slice

Here we can see how information from the eyes gets to the brain.

Visual cortex
the brain processes visual information here

Using other senses

Other parts of the body also supply vital information to the brain that it uses to control body movement. The inner ear, for example, contains three cupulai and three liquid-filled arched tubes called semicircular canals. Together these provide information on movement and help us balance.

Eyes allow us to see where we are and what we are doing, and also give us information on how near or far away objects are from us. People who are blind may rely on their guide dogs to help them to avoid the everyday hazards that sighted people sense with their eyes.

Getting feedback

When the body is moving the brain constantly receives impulses from its different movement and position sensors. The brain then uses this information to send out more commands to fine-tune what the body is doing. This process of fine-tuning happens many times a second. Alcohol and other drugs can cause these signals to slow down and stop this happening properly.

Skateboarder grinding

This skateboarder uses information from many different parts of his body to co-ordinate his movements. These movements have specific names:

Adduction: *moving a part of the body towards the body.*

Abduction: *moving a part of the body away from the body.*

Flexion: *when a joint bends so that the bones come closer together.*

Extension: *when a joint straightens and the bones move further apart.*

The combination of movements enables the skateboarder to perform tricks and stay on his board.

Abduction
for example, flinging the arm out

Ears
help with balance

Flexion
for example, bending the knee

Eyes
provide information on movement

Adduction
for example, pulling the arm into the body

Extension
for example, stretching the leg

Stretch receptors
for example, send impulses to the brain so that the foot stays on the board

LOST IN SPACE?

Here is a way to find out how your body 'senses' where it is. Close your eyes and raise both hands above your head. Keep your left hand totally still.

Now, using your right index finger, quickly touch your nose then reach up and touch the tips of the fingers of your left hand. Repeat the movements, but this time wriggle the fingers of your left hand before moving your right hand.

You should find it easier to touch your fingers the second time. This is because when you wriggle your fingers their stretch receptors provide lots of information to your brain. This helps you locate your fingers even when you cannot see them.

Legs and feet are part of
the walking mechanism

egs are used to make all sorts of powerful movements. Therefore, it is not surprising that some leg movements are controlled by the body's biggest muscle, the gluteus maximus (see pages 10 and 11). The leg also contains the longest and strongest bone in the body – the femur, or thigh bone.

Walking

Walking involves the complex co-ordination of the muscles in the upper and lower leg – that is why it takes such a long time for young children to learn to walk. The muscles in the thigh bend and straighten the leg and move it around the hip joint. The muscles in the lower leg pull the foot up and down and move the toes.

Biceps femoris
bends the leg

Gastrocnemius
bends the foot down

Tibialis anterior
lifts and turns the foot

Soleus
bends the foot down

The leg muscles

Here we can see the main muscles in the leg that provide the pulling force for walking, running, jumping, and even standing still.

The foot

The foot not only supports the body, but also acts as a lever to push it forward (see page 9).

The feet

The feet are a vital part of the walking mechanism. Because of their spring-like arched shape, feet support the weight of the body and help it to balance. They also act as levers to push the body forward. Without feet, walking would be almost impossible. However, developments in artificial limb technology have meant that even people who lose a foot or leg through injury can still lead an active life.

Feet have stretch receptors that send lots of information to the brain about where they are. If this did not happen, we would stumble much more often than we do, especially on uneven surfaces.

Running

Running uses the full power of the leg muscles. Sprinters use their legs to produce explosive movement. Marathon runners use their legs for long sustained effort. Running is a great way for everyone to exercise.

A step forward

Thanks to modern medicine and engineering, artificial limbs let some people who have lost limbs to lead an active life, and play sports such as basketball.

UNDER PRESSURE

You and your friends probably wear running shoes with spongy soles. The shoes are not just there to look good – they also absorb some of the 'shock' of each step you take. This is very important because when you run your feet strike the ground with a force equal to about three times your body weight. If you run on a hard surface without wearing running shoes, almost all of this force is transmitted to the joints and bones in your feet, legs and lower body. This can cause a lot of physical damage.

Arms and hands produce
a variety of movements

Most of the time we use our arms and hands to reach for and to hold things, all without a moment's thought. But we can only do these things because the joints, muscles and bones in our arms and hands can produce a variety of movements.

Using tools

Our long, opposable thumbs allow us to use a variety of tools.

Extensor retinaculum
A 'wrist band' that keeps tendons in place

Abductor pollicis longus
pulls the thumb out to the side

The human thumb

We belong to a group of animals called the primates, most of which have 'opposable' thumbs (the thumb can touch fingers on the same hand). Our long, opposable thumbs allow us to grip things more precisely than other primates. The thumb is opposable because it is connected to the hand by the only 'saddle' joint in the body.

The arm and hand

Forearm muscles produce the movement in the fingers and thumb. If the muscles were in the hand, they would make it too bulky to move properly.

A HANDS-ON EXPERIMENT

You can get a really good clue as to how some of the muscles that work your hand are arranged with this simple experiment.

First put your hand palm down on a table top with the middle finger bent under. Now try and lift your ring finger (the one between the middle and little finger). You will find that it is impossible. This is because the ring finger and middle finger are extended by the same muscle, which can not act when the middle finger is bent. You will be able to lift your other fingers which are extended by other muscles.

Flexor carpi ulnaris .... bends the hand at the wrist

Extensor .... **digitorum** straightens the fingers and the hand

Bend your finger
Our middle and ring fingers are extended by the same muscle.

Arm muscles and hand tendons

When we bend and extend our fingers and thumb, we can see what look like long cords stretching under the skin on the back of the hand and the wrist. These are the tendons of the forearm muscles that connect with bones in the hand.

Tendons of extensor digitorum here you can see that the tendons of the middle and ring finger are connected to the same muscle

A strong grip
The hand can exert a lot of force – enough to crush a drinks can.

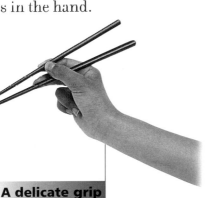

A delicate grip
The hand allows us to make very precise movements, such as holding chopsticks.

Complex structure

The hand is an extremely complex structure – it contains 27 separate bones linked together with muscles, tendons and many intricate joints. This structure allows us to make very fine movements, such as using chopsticks, and very strong movements, such as crushing a drinks can.

People communicate using
facial muscles

The face is capable of an amazing variety of movements that allow us to show, or hide, how we are feeling.

Small movements of the mouth, eyes, eyebrows, nose and other parts of the face show a wide range of human emotions – from anger to happiness. The brain can learn how to tell a person's mood just by looking at the expression on their face. This type of non-verbal (without words) communication helps us interact with people around us.

Frontalis
raises the eyebrows and wrinkles the forehead

Orbicularis oculi
blinks, opens and closes the eyelids

Making a face

Unlike most skeletal muscles, the muscles of the face are not just attached to bones. Most are also attached to the skin and this means that when they move our expression changes – we really do 'pull' a face. We can frown, for example, because of a thin sheet of muscle (frontalis) across the forehead. A circular muscle (orbicularis oris) around the mouth helps control the movements which make us smile and enable us to speak.

Zygomaticus
pulls corners of the mouth upwards in a smile

Masseter
closes the mouth

Buccinator
pulls on the corner of the mouth

Depressor anguli oris
pulls corners of mouth downwards to make face look sad

Mentalis
makes lower lip protrude and wrinkles chin

Orbicularis oris
purses the lips and pushes them out

FACES AND FEELINGS

See how good you are at creating and recognising facial expressions. Use an instant or digital camera to take five pictures of friends making different expressions – each should show a different emotion, for example: fear, happiness, boredom, excitement and anger.

Keep a record of the emotions shown by the pictures. Make a list of the different emotions and swap the pictures among your friends. See if they can match each emotion to the correct picture.

Taking a bite

The skull is made up of 22 bones (there are another six inside the ears). All but one of these skull bones are connected together by rigid joints and form a solid protective case for the brain. Only the bone of the lower jaw (mandible) is joined to the other skull bones by a movable hinge joint. This joint helps us to talk, laugh, and chew food.

Having a look

Six muscles move each eye to point them in the direction we want to look. The brain controls this movement so that both eyes point at the same object. If the eyes could not move, the head would have to turn round, like an owl's, each time we wanted to look at something new.

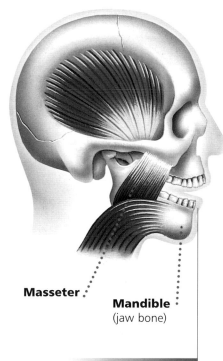

Masseter

Mandible
(jaw bone)

A powerful bite

The muscle that closes the mouth – the masseter muscle – can produce incredible pressures when it moves the mandible (jaw bone) and the teeth bite and chew food.

Looking around

The muscles around the eyes move them so that we can look at things properly.

Exercise helps to
keep the body healthy

Exercise includes everything from playing a game of football to taking a dog out for a walk. In fact, we exercise every time we move. When we do vigorous exercise, such as jogging, the heart starts beating faster and we breathe more quickly. This type of exercise has some very positive effects.

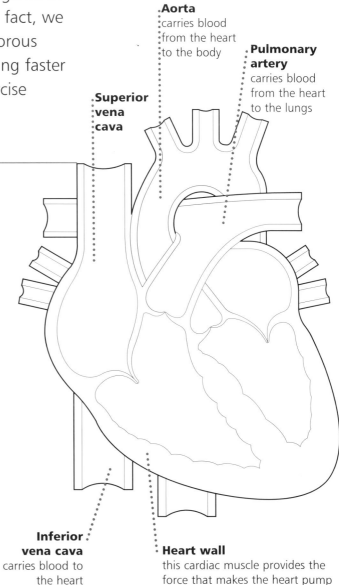

Inside the human heart

The heart pumps blood around the body. The more it is exercised, the better it gets at doing this job. Practise copying and labelling diagrams by tracing this illustration.

Aorta
carries blood from the heart to the body

Pulmonary artery
carries blood from the heart to the lungs

Superior vena cava

Inferior vena cava
carries blood to the heart

Heart wall
this cardiac muscle provides the force that makes the heart pump

Stamina

If we exercise regularly then the heart muscle gets stronger, which makes it better at pumping blood around the body. The muscles that move the lungs are also strengthened, allowing more oxygen to pass into the blood. These are just two of the ways that exercise makes the body better at supplying oxygen to the muscles. In turn, we get more stamina.

Building muscles

Strength training makes muscles bigger by putting them under stress — as they recover they grow bigger.

Strength

Exercise can also make us stronger. This happens especially when we do exercises that put our muscles under stress, for example when we lift weights. When muscles recover from this stress their fibres get bigger and this makes them stronger and more powerful. However, lifting weights that are too heavy, or lifting them incorrectly, can cause serious muscle strain.

BLOOD FLOW TO THE BODY

This diagram shows how much blood flows per minute to different parts of the body when a person is at rest and when they are exercising. As you can see, exercise greatly increases the amount of blood reaching the muscles – this is so they get enough oxygen.

Location	At rest	During exercise
a Muscles	1 litre	12 litres
b Coronary arteries of heart	0.25 litre	0.75 litre
c Brain	0.25 litre	0.25 litre
d Kidneys	0.75 litre	0.75 litre
e Digestive system	1.5 litres	0.5 litre
f Skin	0.5 litre	2 litres

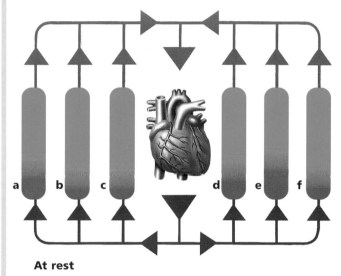

At rest

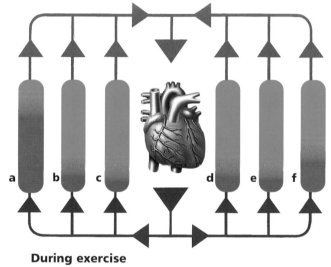

During exercise

Fitness

As well as giving us stamina and making us stronger, exercise can also make us more flexible, improve our health and make us less likely to fall ill.

Exercise also uses a lot of energy. It can help us 'burn off' the excess energy in the body, which is stored as fat, and so help us slim down. In fact, the more we move the fitter we become, although the body does need to have rest and to replace used energy.

Getting fit

Exercise is not only good for you, but it is also great fun.

The body can stop
moving properly

Movement involves many different parts of the body, many of which are complex and delicate, and it is easy to take it for granted. However, many things can happen that stop us moving or make movement very difficult. Problems can be caused by overuse, accidents or disease.

Muscle problems

Many sportsmen and women strain or 'tear' their muscles when they put them under too much stress. They can also suffer from cramp. This happens when a muscle contracts sharply and does not relax. Cramp is caused by overexertion or too much heat or cold. If muscles are not used enough, for example when a leg is set in plaster because of a broken bone, then the muscle fibres can atrophy (get smaller and weaker). This can be a problem for astronauts who spend long periods of time in zero gravity, as their muscles can waste away.

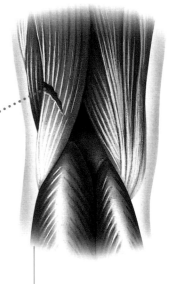

Biceps femoris this type of 'hamstring' injury can cause internal bleeding

Hamstring injury
Here we can see a torn hamstring, an injury that often happens to sprinters and football players.

Torn Achilles tendon
This injury often requires surgery to reconnect the tendon to the heel.

Elbow the elbow contains a hinge joint

Tender tendons
The tendons linking the forearm muscles to the elbow can become sore if the joint is overworked.

Achilles tendon the Achilles tendon was named after an Ancient Greek warrior who could only be hurt in this part of his foot

Wear and tear

Joints and tendons are particularly vulnerable to injury. For example, the bursae in the knee joint often get inflamed if the knees are overused – this is called 'housemaid's knee'. The tendon that links the forearm muscles to the elbow can become sore if the arm is used too much – this is often called 'tennis elbow'.

Disease and illness

As we get older our bodies can start to break down. Many old people suffer from arthritis. This is a disease which affects joints and makes them difficult to move. Some diseases, injuries and illnesses badly damage nerves and slow down or prevent movement. For example, damage to the spinal cord may cause paralysis below the level of the injury.

Arthritic hands

As we get older, diseases such as arthritis can make it difficult and painful to move.

LOOK AFTER YOUR BODY

A balanced diet and regular exercise are very important if you want to look after your body and keep it moving. You can look after your muscles and joints in many other ways, too. It is very important, for example, to stretch muscles properly by 'warming up' before exercising, and by 'warming down' afterwards. How you move, sit and lift heavy loads is also crucial – if you do these things incorrectly you can cause all sorts of problems in your muscles and joints.

Warming up

Stretching muscles before exercising is very important if we want to prevent painful injuries.

Glossary

Actin A thin protein filament found inside muscle myofibrils. Actin acts together with myosin to cause myofibrils to contract.

Arthritis A disease that often afflicts the elderly. It causes inflammation of the joints and restricts movement.

ATP A high energy substance that stores energy inside the cell until it is needed.

Bursae Sacs of fluid found within some synovial joints. These help cushion joints and make movement smoother.

Carbohydrate An important part of our diets, carbohydrates are a key source of energy. Carbohydrates are found in food such as bread, potatoes and sugar.

Cardiac muscle Muscle found in the heart that produces the heartbeat. Cardiac muscle contracts on its own without tiring.

Cartilage Tissue that protects the ends of bones and acts as a shock-absorber. Found, for example, inside the knee joints.

Fascicle Bundle of muscle fibres held together with a sheath. A skeletal muscle is made up of many fascicles.

Filament The tiny threads inside a myofibril. There are two types of filament – actin and myosin – that act together to make a myofibril contract.

Flexibility The ability to move, bend and stretch the limbs and body without injury.

Glucose A type of carbohydrate used as a source of energy by the body.

Lever A simple machine comprising a rod and fulcrum that is used to transfer force.

Mitochondria Microscopic structures within cells where the energy released from glucose is used to form ATP.

Muscle A type of body tissue that can contract and relax and therefore create movement within the body.

Muscle fibre A microscopic threadlike structure that is the basic muscle unit or cell. Each has the ability to contract and relax.

Myofibril A microscopic thread inside muscle fibres. Myofibrils contain filaments of actin and myosin – the structures that make muscles contract.

Myosin A thick protein filament found inside myofibrils. Myosin acts together with actin to cause myofibrils to contract.

Nerve A bundle of long specialised cells that carry electrical signals called nerve impulses.

Nerve impulse An electrical signal that travels along a nerve.

Protein An essential part of the diet found in food such as meat, eggs and cheese. Protein is used to build muscles, skin and many other structures in the body.

Reflex action A split-second automatic response by the body to a strong stimulus such as heat. It occurs without the direct involvement of the brain.

Respiration The process by which the energy released from food is used to form ATP. Aerobic respiration occurs in mitochondria and needs oxygen. Anaerobic respiration does not.

Skeletal muscles Muscles that pull on the bones of the skeleton to move the body. They also keep the body upright, maintain posture and give the body its shape. They are under the conscious control of the brain.

Smooth muscle Muscle found in the walls of hollow organs such as the bladder and blood vessels. It contracts without us thinking about it.

Stamina The ability to perform a physical activity for a long period of time.

Synovial fluid Fluid that lubricates synovial joints. It is produced by the synovial membrane that lines the joint cavity.

Synovial joint A movable joint that is lubricated by synovial fluid.

Tendon A tough cord made up of collagen fibres that connects a muscle to a bone.

Thermogram A 'heat picture' taken using equipment sensitive to infra-red radiation. It can show how hot different parts of the body are in relation to each other.

Find out more

These are just some of the websites where you can find out more information about how we move. Many of the websites also provide information and illustrations about other systems and processes of the human body.

Note to parents and teachers
Every effort has been made by the Publishers to ensure that these websites are suitable for children; that they are of the highest educational value, and that they contain no inappropriate or offensive material. However, because of the nature of the Internet, it is impossible to guarantee that the contents of these sites will not be altered. We strongly advise that Internet access is supervised by a responsible adult.

www.bbc.co.uk/health/kids
Find out how to keep fit and healthy on this website from the BBC. There are great sections on exercising, diet and sport.

www.howstuffworks.com
Go to the 'science stuff' section of this site for lots of information on how muscles and other parts of the body work. A great place to look if you want to find out more.

www.ich.ucl.ac.uk/ kidsandteens/index.html
Visit the website of the world-famous Great Ormond Street Hospital for Children to find out lots about how doctors can help make us better. You'll find a great 'body tour' and you can even email in questions.

www.exploratorium.edu
Lots of stuff on science, including the science of sports.

www.ajkids.com
A search engine for asking questions about science – just type in your query, press return and you'll be shown where to get the best answer.

www.brainpop.com/health
Find out all about the body, including lots on the muscular system and fitness. You can even download an animated movie of the muscular system in action.

www.kidshealth.org
Find out information about all the different parts of your body and how to keep them healthy. Includes a great section on 'your multi-talented muscles'.

www.bbc.co.uk/sport
Keep up to date with what's happening in the world of sport, where some of the world's best movers are in action!

www.learn.co.uk
A website from the Guardian newspaper aimed at both students and teachers. This covers everything you need for the national curriculum on the body, movement and health.

www.bbc.co.uk/science/ humanbody
Another site devoted to the parts of the body and how they work – find out more about muscles, the skeleton, the nervous system and how they produce movement.

www.abc.net.au/science
The Lab – an Australian website that has lots of exciting features and up-to-date news items about different science subjects, including health.

Index